YOUR DREAM HOME

AN ESSENTIAL GUIDE FOR HOME BUYERS

I0517898

JEREMY WILLIAMS

WWW.TRUEVINEPUBLISHING.ORG

Your Dream Home
By Jeremy Williams

Published by
True Vine Publishing Co.
810 Dominican Dr.
Nashville, TN 37228
www.TrueVinePublishing.org

Copyright © 2025 by Jeremy Williams
ISBN: 978-1-962783-96-5 Paperback
ISBN: 978-1-962783-97-2 ebook

Printed in the United States of America—First printing.

Foreword

First and foremost, thank you. By choosing to delve into this book, you're not just embracing a guide but inviting a dance partner for one of life's most exhilarating and deeply personal journeys: finding a place to call home.

Crafting this guide has been a dance in its own right. A waltz through experiences, a tango with tales, and a foxtrot with the finest details of home buying and cherishing. But, like any dance, it's infinitely richer when shared. Your presence, gives this narrative its purpose and rhythm.

As you cha-cha through these chapters, it's entirely possible you'll have questions, musings, or perhaps a wee bit of feedback (be it applause or constructive critique, both are welcomed in equal measure). Please remember, this isn't just a monologue. It's a conversation, a partnership.

Should any queries pirouette through your mind or if you just fancy a good old chinwag about homes, dreams, or the art of the perfect jive, I'm merely a call, text, or email away

This journey we're about to embark upon is illuminated by your aspirations, challenges, and victories. Every story, every experience, enriches the narrative. So, don't hesitate to reach out. Think of me as your dance instructor, ready to guide, assist, and occasionally share a hearty chuckle.

To the wondrous dance ahead and the tales yet to unfold, let's sway, leap, and twirl together into the magical world of homes and heartbeats.

With gratitude and a spring in my step, let's make every step count! Download my contact details to your phone using this QR Code, and click the "Add To Contacts" button:

Jeremy Williams

Table of Contents

Foreword 3

Introduction 7

CHAPTER 1 The Tantalizing Tango of Taking the Plunge 9

CHAPTER 2 The Sizzling Salsa of Seeking Support...........13

CHAPTER 3 The Waltz of Wisdom and Wants 16

CHAPTER 4 The Riveting Rumba of Realty Negotiations 19

CHAPTER 5 The Fabulous Foxtrot of Finalizing the Deal 22

CHAPTER 6 The Jubilant Jive of Jumping In 25

CHAPTER 7 The Sizzling Samba of Settling In 28

CHAPTER 8 The Waltz of Wisdom and Wonder.................31

EPILOGUE The Grand Finale - A Dance for the Ages......34

Appendixes 37

Introduction

The Enigma of a Dream Home

In the grand tapestry of life, there exists an age-old mystery, whispered among generations, sought by many, and unlocked by only a handful. The quest? The perfect home. Not just bricks and beams, but a sanctuary of dreams, desires, and memories. A place where walls absorb laughter, floors echo footsteps of reunions, and windows open to horizons of hope.

Welcome, dear reader, to the heart-pounding, nail-biting journey of "HOME PURCHASE - UNLOCK SECRETS TO SUCCESSFUL HOME OWNERSHIP." A journey where the codes to flawless home-buying are decrypted, and the veiled paths to creating an oasis of comfort are unveiled.

Ever wondered why some glide through the property market like seasoned dancers, while others stumble and falter? Why, for some, the doors of their dream homes swing open effortlessly, while others remain forever in search, keys jingling in vain? The answers, my friend, are woven into the pages that lie ahead.

In this volume, not only will we decode the mysteries of the real estate realm, but we'll also embark on a thrilling voyage—past the siren calls of swanky showrooms, through the labyrinthine alleys of legalese, over the shifting sands of market trends, to the serene shores of successful home ownership.

But, be forewarned: this isn't just another property manual. It's a pulsating, edge-of-your-seat adventure. Each chapter, a new revelation. Every tip, a stepping stone to mastering the rhythm and choreography of the real estate waltz.

So, fasten your seat belts, grip the edges of this tome, and prepare for an exhilarating roller-coaster through the enigma of owning your dream space. The secrets? Well, they're about to be laid bare.

Are you ready to unlock the doors to your dreams?

CHAPTER 1

The Tantalizing Tango of Taking the Plunge

The sun streamed through the blinds, casting golden streaks on the wooden table. There you sat, coffee in one hand, a dream in your mind, and your heart in... someone else's house? Yup, that's right! Sarah might've been the one noticing that "For Sale" sign today, but guess what? You've been doing the exact same thing during your morning commutes.

Ever found yourself daydreaming about a home with a walk-in closet big enough to get lost in? Or maybe a backyard where the only thing you're tripping over is the natural beauty (and not those pesky toys)? Welcome to the club!

The thought starts innocently enough. "Oh, isn't that house cute? I wonder what it's like inside." And before you know it, you're 47 pages deep into a Zillow spiral at 2 am, thinking, "Could I pull off a sunroom? I mean, I do like sun. And rooms."

Your First Move: Dancing with Desire

Ah, desire. It's that sneaky little emotion that starts with an innocent glance and ends with you Googling "How to buy a home without losing my mind?" It begins subtly. Maybe it's the pitter-patter of tiny feet on the horizon. Perhaps it's the not-so-subtle nudges from your partner about needing more space. Or maybe you're just fed up with your current digs because, frankly, your neighbor's fascination with experimental jazz flute at 3 am is wearing thin.

But then you ask yourself, "Do I really want to go through the hoops and hurdles of buying a home?" Heck, you've heard the stories. And here's where your brain starts its classic tango of 'Should I, shouldn't I?'

Now, Pause and Reflect

Before the allure of double sinks and walk-in pantries completely hypnotizes you, take a moment. Grab a notebook, your favorite pen, and maybe a glass of wine (or two, no judgments here), and let's break this down.

1. What's Your "Why"?

Is it space? Investment? A desire to finally have a place where no landlord can judge your choice of neon green as a bathroom color? (You go, avant-garde Picasso!)

2.Internet Stalk Houses

Dive into those online real estate platforms. Oh, come on. We know you've bookmarked them. Scroll through. Lust after. Get your virtual feet wet.

3.Credit Score Check

Okay, time to face the music. And not the jazz flute kind. Knowing your score is like knowing your dance moves. Essential for impressing...well, the bank.

4.Budgeting

We're not saying you should skip that fancy coffee, but knowing what you're working with is critical. 'Cause while a house made entirely of chocolate sounds amazing, you might want to ensure you can pay for the non-edible kind first.

5.Learn, Learn, Learn

Webinars, workshops, podcasts. Become a sponge. And not the kind you use to clean up after spilling that wine we mentioned earlier.

6.Chit-Chat

Talk to people who've done this dance before. Trust us, their tales of property triumphs (and mishaps) will be both enlightening and entertaining.

Concluding this Cha-Cha

You might wonder, why on earth would you willingly dive into the world of escrows, inspections, and bidding wars? Maybe it's the prospect of building a legacy. Perhaps it's the thought of hosting epic holiday dinners. Or possibly, just possibly, it's about proving to yourself that you can tackle one of adulthood's most iconic challenges and emerge, keys in hand, like the rockstar you are.

By the end of this chapter, here's our promise to you: You'll be well-equipped, well-informed, and, hopefully, chuckling at the delightful chaos that is the home-buying experience. So, strap in! This is going to be one thrilling ride. And remember, even if you trip during this tango, we're here to help you find your rhythm again. Now, shall we dance?

CHAPTER 2

The Sizzling Salsa of Seeking Support

You've danced the tango of desire and you're ready for your next move. Now it's time to learn the salsa – a passionate dance that requires a partner. And when it comes to home buying, this partner is the one who guides, supports, and occasionally steps on your toes: your real estate agent.

The journey from desire to reality is kind of like salsa dancing on a crowded floor. You need someone to lead you through the crowd, help you keep the rhythm, and ensure you don't get elbowed in the face. That, my friend, is where a real estate agent comes into play.

Finding Your Fred Astaire (or Ginger Rogers)

Before diving headfirst into the exhilarating world of open houses, MLS databases, and escrow accounts, you need a guide. Think of your agent as the experienced salsa dancer who knows every twirl, dip, and shimmy needed to make the journey smooth and, dare we say, enjoyable?

But how do you find this mythical creature?

Agent Interviews: The First Date

Referrals and Recommendations: Remember those chit-chats from chapter one? Yep, time to revisit. Ask your friends, families, and even that random coworker about agents they've worked with.

Experience Matters: This isn't their first rodeo, and it shouldn't be. You want someone with the experience to tackle anything the market might throw at you.

Specialized Knowledge: If you're after that chic downtown condo, maybe don't choose an agent who specializes in rural barn conversions.

Vibe Check: Your agent is someone you're going to be working closely with. If their idea of a "cozy cottage" looks more like Dracula's lair to you, it's perhaps not a match made in real estate heaven.

Shimmying through Listings and Locations

With your real estate agent by your side, it's time to explore.

1. Priorities, Darling: Make a list. Check it twice. Your agent isn't a mind reader. If a sunroom is non-negotiable for your dream home, say it loud and proud.

2. Open House Hustle: Visit. A lot. Open houses are like free salsa lessons. Sometimes awkward, often enlightening, but always an experience.

3. Location, Location, Cha-Cha-Cha: Always loved the east side? Great! But let your agent show you a surprise or two. Maybe there's a neighborhood you've never considered that's actually a hidden gem.

The Dip at the End

Finding and working with an agent is a partnership. It's a sultry dance, where communication is the music and trust is the rhythm. So put on those dancing shoes, and let's salsa our way to your dream home!

And remember, in this salsa of home buying, it's okay if you sometimes step on your partner's toes. Just laugh it off, adjust your step, and keep moving. The dance floor of real estate is vast, but with the right partner, every step can be a celebration. Now, ready to turn up the heat in chapter 3?

CHAPTER 3

The Waltz of Wisdom and Wants

If the tango had you introspecting and the salsa got you seeking, then the waltz is about finding balance and harmony. You're not just prancing around on a ballroom floor here; you're juggling desires, needs, and good old-fashioned wisdom. Let's face it, when it comes to homes, what we want and what we need sometimes feels like ordering a diet soda with a triple cheeseburger. But hey, it's about balance!

Strutting into the Specifics

With your trusty real estate agent at your side (who's definitely proved they can lead without stepping on your feet), it's time to drill down into the nitty-gritty.

Reality Check-In: You've probably envisioned your dream house a million times: the bay windows, the sprawling gardens, that unnecessarily large but oh-so-fancy marble bathtub. But remember: some dreams fit perfectly into our reality, and some are better suited for when we win the lottery.

Location Lovers: You loved the east side. You were open to some surprises. Now, after a series of tours and discussions, it's time to get definitive. What's it gonna be? The lively buzz of downtown, the serene burbs, or the charming outskirts? Each has its own rhythm in the waltz of house hunting.

Budget Bounce: By now, you've got a clearer idea of what your money can get you. It's like shopping for shoes – sometimes you're in the designer section, sometimes you're hunting for deals, and sometimes you find that unexpected gem that's both stunning and surprisingly affordable.

Fine-Tuning Your Footwork

With each house you view, you'll refine your wants. And with each discussion with your agent, you'll gain wisdom.

Future-Proofing: Maybe you're a party of two now, but what about in five years? If you hear the faint tick of a biological or ambition clock, it's worth considering what spaces you might need in the future.

Investment Intellect: Sure, it's your home, but it's also an investment. Think about the resale value. Are there upcoming developments in the area that might boost property values?

Wants vs. Needs: That game room sounds amazing,

doesn't it? But if it comes at the expense of essential living space, it might be worth reconsidering. Remember our diet soda and cheeseburger analogy? Balance.

The Graceful Glide

The waltz of home buying is a dance of elegance. It's where dreams meet decisions, and desires shake hands with reality. As you glide through this step, cherish the memories you're making. Each viewing, each discussion is a step closer to your dream home.

And as the melody of this chapter fades and you're left in the embrace of your desires and wisdom, remember: the dance floor is vast, but with every step, turn, and twirl, you're painting a story that's uniquely yours. Ready to step into the rumba of negotiations in the next chapter?

CHAPTER 4

The Riveting Rumba of Realty Negotiations

Welcome to the rumba! This isn't just any old dance; it's the one where tensions rise, palms get sweaty, and the stakes are higher than ever. But just like any great rumba dancer knows, it's all about feeling the rhythm, understanding your partner, and making those moves with conviction.

Entering the Negotiation Arena

As you sashay into this stage with your agent (who's now feeling more like a battle-hardened comrade than a dance partner), it's time to face the sellers. Whether it's a straight-faced couple who believe their house is the next Buckingham Palace or a delightful old lady who's just looking for the right people to cherish her beloved abode, negotiations are never one-size-fits-all.

Starting the Dance: Your first offer sets the tone. You've got your budget, but remember – this is a dance of back-and-forth, of give and take. Start wisely, but be ready for some sassy footwork.

Reading the Room(ba): The seller's counteroffer will tell you a lot. Are they in a hurry to sell? Do they think their house is plated in gold? Or are they just testing the waters? Whatever it is, it's time for you to match their steps with precision.

Contingencies and Clauses: These are your dance moves, your steps. Need the sale to be contingent on your old home selling? Want to ensure the cracked window is fixed before you move in? Make sure to put on your dancing shoes and lay out your terms.

Stepping, Sliding, and Sometimes Stumbling

Look, not every step in the rumba is going to be perfect. You might face rejection, a counter you weren't expecting, or even discover some undisclosed flaws in the home.

Home Inspections: Think of this as a dance rehearsal. A professional comes in, checks out the house's every nook and cranny, and ensures you're not buying a lemon. If there are hidden defects, it's time to either renegotiate or decide if it's a deal-breaker.

Stay Calm and Rumba On: There'll be moments of tension, moments when you'll want to stomp off the dance floor. But remember, keep your cool. You've got this, and your agent is right there with you.

The Power of Walking Away: Sometimes, the rhythm just isn't right. If a deal isn't aligning with your needs, it might be time to step away gracefully and find a new dance floor.

The Final Flourish

The rumba of negotiations is all about passion and patience. It's a dance where emotions run high, and every move can make or break the deal. But remember, every step, even the missteps, are all part of the journey.

As the music slows and you await the seller's response, it's a mix of anxiety and exhilaration. Did your moves impress? Did you strike the right chord? As the curtain falls on this chapter, remember: whether this negotiation leads to a successful purchase or another round of house hunting, you're learning, growing, and becoming a maestro in the great dance of home buying. So, shall we foxtrot into the world of finalizing in the next chapter?

CHAPTER 5

The Fabulous Foxtrot of Finalizing the Deal

Ah, the foxtrot! A dance of fluid movements, subtle nuances, and an air of sophistication. Just when you thought the rumba was the crescendo, you realize that there's a final, elegant dance to perform: finalizing your home purchase. This isn't just a dance; it's your standing ovation.

Taking the Stage with Grace

You've negotiated, you've adjusted, and now it's time to sign on the dotted line. But the performance isn't over yet.

Mortgage Magic: Securing the right mortgage can feel a bit like mastering a particularly tricky dance step. There are terms to be understood, rates to be locked in, and paperwork that seems to rival the height of Everest. But with the right lender, it feels less like a tedious task and more like a graceful glide across the floor.

The Appraisal Pirouette: Your chosen house needs

to be appraised to ensure the price matches its value. Imagine this as a judge's score in a dance competition. Too high, and you're over the moon. Too low, and there might be some more negotiations or reevaluations to be done.

Title Tango: Making sure the title of the house is clear is essential. No liens, no disputes. It's like ensuring no one else claims they had the winning dance performance. This is your stage now!

Bowing to the Audience (and Crossing the Ts)

While the spotlight shines bright, there are a few more steps to ensure a flawless finish.

Home Insurance Interlude: Before you take the final bow, ensure your new stage (aka your home) is protected from any unexpected events. Fires, floods, alien invasions? Maybe not the last one, but it's always good to be covered.

Final Walk-through Waltz: One last dance in your soon-to-be home. Check if everything is as agreed. Are the repairs done? Has the house been maintained since your last visit? This is your final rehearsal before the main event.

Closing Crescendo: The papers are ready, the keys are jingling, and it's time to sign, seal, and deliver. The house is yours! With every signature, you can almost hear the applause getting louder.

The Encore

As the music comes to its triumphant end, you find yourself in the center of the stage – your new home. The journey, with all its steps, twirls, and occasional missteps, has been nothing short of spectacular. And like any great performance, it was made better with a partner – your ever-reliable real estate agent.

As the curtain descends on this chapter, you might find yourself reminiscing about the dance that was. And just wait until you swing into the next phase: decorating! But that, dear reader, is a story (and dance) for another time.

Feeling the rhythm in your bones and ready to jive into your new journey of homeownership? Let's embark on that in the next chapter!

CHAPTER 6

The Jubilant Jive of Jumping In

The curtains rise, the lights are bright, and the audience is ecstatic. Welcome to the jive, where everything is energetic, quick-paced, and joyful! With the paperwork behind you, it's now time to leap into your new home with both feet and truly make it your own.

Embarking on the Homecoming Hustle

Stepping into your new home is a rush of emotions: excitement, pride, maybe a hint of nerves. But mostly, there's an undeniable sense of accomplishment.

Moving Mambo: Now comes the dance of moving in. Boxes stacked like building blocks, furniture shuffled around like puzzle pieces, and a choreography that involves dodging rogue toys and misplaced mugs. You might step on a few toes (or Lego pieces) but remember, it's all part of the rhythm.

Decorative Disco: Those blank walls are your canvas.

Maybe you're thinking lavish Renaissance art, or perhaps, modern abstracts are more your groove. Whatever your style, it's time to splash it all over your new home. Get your groove on with paints, fixtures, and fittings.

Neighborhood Networking: Now that you've moved into the neighborhood, it's time to meet the locals. Think of it as expanding your dance troupe. A friendly hello, a shared cup of sugar, or perhaps joining the local salsa class (why not keep the dance theme going?).

Twirling Through Triumphs and Tiny Troubles

Every jive has its high jumps and rapid kicks. It's fun, but it's not without its challenges.

Home Improvement Hustle: That squeaky floorboard, the slightly drippy faucet, the mysterious light switch that appears to do absolutely nothing? Time to roll up those sleeves and embark on the DIY journey, or maybe call in the pros for a more complex gig.

Garden Groove: Whether you have a sprawling backyard or a quaint balcony, there's always room to get your hands dirty. Plant some flowers, set up a hammock, or maybe even build that treehouse you always dreamed of as a kid.

The Unforeseen Two-step: Maybe it's a sudden leak during the first rain or a missing mailbox. Houses, like any good dance partner, can sometimes throw a surprise step your way. But with a bit of agility and a can-do spirit, you'll be back in sync in no time.

A Standing Ovation

As you settle into the groove of your new home, it becomes more than just walls and a roof. It becomes the stage for countless memories, endless dances, and life's beautiful choreography.

With every laugh shared, every meal cooked, and every night spent under its shelter, the bond with your home deepens. And through it all, the jive continues – vibrant, spirited, and full of life.

Take a moment to bask in the applause (even if it's just from your pet or a proud plant you've managed not to kill). You've danced through the challenging steps of homeownership and have emerged, twirling with joy in your very own space.

Feeling the beat pick up again? Ready for the next rhythm of making this house truly a home? Strap on those dancing shoes, and let's cha-cha into the future!

CHAPTER 7

The Sizzling Samba of Settling In

L ights dim. The atmosphere pulsates with anticipation. As the samba's beat resonates, you find yourself not just in a home, but a lived-in space that mirrors your essence. This chapter is all about relishing the moments, enjoying the nuances, and truly settling in.

Immersing in the Melody of Memories

From empty rooms echoing with potential to a cozy abode filled with life's little moments, this dance is all about savoring.

Host the Housewarming Hustle: Celebrate your new home with a flair. Whether it's an intimate dinner or a lively party where everyone does the conga, your home's warmth gets amplified with loved ones around.

Nooks and Niches Nightingale: Discover your home's little quirks. That sunlit corner perfect for reading. The kitchen spot that's inexplicably cooler. Every home sings a unique tune. Listen closely.

Culture and Community Cha-Cha: Explore your surroundings. Maybe there's a coffee shop that plays jazz on Sundays or a park where families fly kites. Dive deep into the culture of your new locale.

Swaying with Serendipity and Solutions

Every samba has its swerves. As you find your rhythm in your new abode, remember, it's a dance that keeps evolving.

Crisis Calypso: That moment when you realize you've misplaced your favorite mug or when the heater decides to play coy in winter. It's the dance of quick fixes and finding joy in solutions.

Bonding Bolero: Bond with your neighbors. Maybe it's through a shared love for gardening or a joint yard sale. These connections often form the support system in times of need and celebrations alike.

Sustainability Swing: Now that you're settled, consider the long game. Maybe it's time to think solar panels or a kitchen garden. How can your home dance in harmony with nature?

The Encore of Everyday Euphoria

As days transform into nights and seasons come and go, the samba continues. Your once new house is now filled with echoes of laughter, contemplative silences, and memories woven into every brick.

The magic isn't just in the milestones but in the everyday moments. That feeling when you sip coffee gazing out of your window, the warmth of your favorite blanket, or the contented sigh when you sink into your couch after a long day.

Through highs and lows, quick beats and slow tempos, your home stands as a testament to your journey. The dance of settling in is a continuous one, filled with grace, love, and a touch of whimsy.

As you twirl in the embrace of your home, remember, the dance floor is vast, and there's always a new step to learn, a new tune to hum. So, lace up, and let's waltz into tomorrow with joy and anticipation!

CHAPTER 8

The Waltz of Wisdom and Wonder

In a softly lit ballroom, the melodic strains of a piano float in the air. The waltz – a dance of elegance, composure, and insight. As you transition from the fast-paced samba of settling in, step 8 invites you to reflect, grow, and savor the deep connection with your home.

Dancing with Deeper Understanding

Having lived in your home for a while now, you've gathered stories, secrets, and a profound sense of belonging.

Reflection Rumba: Take a moment, perhaps in the tranquility of a morning or the peace of an evening, to ponder upon the journey so far. The challenges faced, the victories celebrated, and the infinite moments that make up the tapestry of your home life.

Maintenance Minuet: With time, every home needs a touch-up, a polish, a tweak. Maybe it's that creaky stair or the slightly fading wall paint in the bedroom. With grace and care, you dance the minuet, ensuring your home retains its charm and function.

Wisdom Waltz: Sharing is caring. Now, as a seasoned homeowner, perhaps you can offer guidance to a newbie. Offer tips, share stories, or simply lend a listening ear.

Grooving with Gratitude and Growth

The lessons of a home are many, from practical knowledge to deep, personal insights.

Gratitude Groove: Every corner of your house has a story. Be it the living room that witnessed family movie nights or the balcony that became the backdrop for many a contemplative evening. Embrace the gratitude for these spaces and the memories they harbor.

Learning Lindy Hop: No matter how long you've been in your home, there's always something new to discover or learn. Maybe it's a DIY repair or understanding sustainable living better. The dance of knowledge never stops.

Evolving Ensemble: As life evolves, so might your needs from your home. A new family member, a work-from-home setup, or perhaps a newfound hobby. Adapt and adjust, ensuring your home resonates with your life's current tune.

The Symphony of Sentiment

As the notes of the waltz softly fade, a profound realization dawns. Home isn't just about bricks and beams; it's about hopes and dreams. The journey of home ownership, with its myriad dances, has now transitioned into a waltz of wisdom – a dance that marries experience with anticipation.

With every passing day, your bond with your home deepens, becoming a silent witness to your life's ever-evolving dance. As you glide through the ballroom of life, with your home as your steadfast partner, the dance continues, filled with grace, growth, and boundless wonder.

What comes next in this grand dance of life and home? Only time will tell. But for now, let's savor the beauty of the waltz and the profound connection we've nurtured with the space we call home. Join me, dear reader, as we two-step into the future, ready for whatever tune life plays next!

EPILOGUE

The Grand Finale - A Dance for the Ages

The curtain falls, the music softly ebbs, and as we take our final bow, it's with a heart full of gratitude and rooms bursting with memories. Our journey, dear reader, through the majestic ballroom of home buying and ownership, has been one of rhythm, resilience, and remarkable revelations.

From the first timid steps of consideration to the flamboyant flair of final settlement, we've tangoed through trials, waltzed amidst wisdom, and jived with jubilation. Each chapter, each dance step, brought with it a new lesson, a fresh perspective, and tales that are as varied as they are universal.

Yet, homes are not just structures; they are soulful sanctuaries. Beyond the bricks, beams, and borrowed sugar, homes are where our stories unfold, where our dreams take flight, and where love finds its coziest corner.

In this dance of discovery, we've not only found our

dream homes but also uncovered parts of ourselves. We've laughed at the foibles, winced at the missteps, cheered for the victories, and perhaps even shed a tear or two at the profound moments of connection.

And as with any good dance, it's not about perfection, but expression. It's about the journey, not just the destination. It's the laughter, the stumbles, the get-up-and-try-agains, and the quiet moments of reflection amidst the whirlwind waltz of life.

As we close this book, let's not see it as the end but as a sparkling transition. For every homeowner, the dance continues. New rooms to decorate, walls that demand a fresh coat of paint, and gardens that beckon with the promise of bloom.

And for you, dear reader, armed with the insights, stories, and cheeky advice from these pages, may your home be more than just a place to live. May it be a canvas of memories, a fortress of solace, and a stage for life's grandest performances.

So, here's to you and your dance with destiny! As you twirl through life, may your home always echo with melodies of joy, love, and endless wonder.

Keep dancing, keep dreaming, and remember: every home has its own rhythm. All you have to do is listen and dance along.

Until our next dance, keep your steps light and your hearts lighter. Adieu!

Appendixes

The Home Buying Checklist

1. Considering a Property Purchase

Research Goals:

☐ Identify the reasons for wanting to buy a home.

☐ Make a list of essential features you want in a home.

☐ Decide on the preferred type of property (e.g., single-family, condo, townhouse).

Financial Assessment:

☐ Check your credit score and resolve any outstanding issues.

☐ Determine your budget range.

☐ Calculate potential monthly mortgage payments.

☐ Save for a down payment.

☐ Set aside money for closing costs and other unexpected expenses.

Preliminary Research:

☐ Start following real estate trends in desired areas.

☐ Attend local open houses to get a feel for the market.

☐ Begin networking with real estate professionals.

2. Choosing a Real Estate Agent

Research:

☐ Ask friends and family for agent recommendations.

☐ Check online reviews and testimonials.

☐ Look for agents with expertise in your desired location and property type.

Initial Consultation:

☐ Schedule meetings with potential agents.

☐ Discuss your property goals and preferences.

☐ Ask about the agent's experience and past successes.

Finalize Agreement:

☐ Select an agent.

☐ Sign a buyer's agent agreement.

☐ Set communication preferences and frequency.

3. Searching for Properties

Needs and Wants:

☐ Distinguish between must-have and nice-to-have features.

☐ Identify preferred neighborhoods or regions.

Online Searches:

☐ Set up property alerts for your criteria.

☐ Regularly browse listings.

☐ Make a list of potential properties.

Property Visits:

☐ Schedule visits with your agent.

☐ Take notes during showings.

☐ Discuss likes and dislikes after each visit.

4. Making an Offer

Research Comparable Properties:

☐ Determine an offer price based on similar properties.

☐ Understand current market dynamics (e.g., seller's market vs. buyer's market).

Draft the Offer:

☐ Determine contingencies (e.g., inspection, financing).

☐ Decide on the initial deposit amount.

☐ Set a closing date.

Negotiations:

☐ Be prepared for counteroffers.

☐ Discuss and adjust terms with your agent's guidance.

5. Under Contract

Inspection:

☐ Hire a professional inspector.

☐ Attend the inspection.

☐ Review the inspection report and negotiate repairs or credits.

Finalize Financing:

☐ Lock in a mortgage rate.

☐ Submit all required documentation to the lender.

☐ Obtain mortgage approval.

Prepare for Closing:

☐ Conduct a final walkthrough.

☐ Confirm all repairs were completed.

☐ Set up utilities for the new property.

6. Closing

Review Documents:

☐ Ensure all terms match your understanding.

☐ Verify all fees and charges.

☐ Check details like property boundaries.

Sign Documents:

☐ Bring necessary identification.

☐ Ensure funds are available for closing costs and down payment.

Obtain Keys:

☐ Coordinate key handover with the seller or agent.

7. Settling In

Move-In:

☐ Hire reputable movers or organize a DIY move.

☐ Update your address with necessary parties (e.g., post office, utilities).

Home Setup:

☐ Purchase necessary furnishings.

☐ Set up safety measures like alarms or security systems.

☐ Make any desired changes or renovations.

Meet the Neighbors:

☐ Introduce yourself.

☐ Attend or organize neighborhood gatherings.

8. Reflect and Share

Maintenance:

☐ Create a regular maintenance schedule.

☐ Address any issues that arise.

Community Involvement:

☐ Get involved in local activities or organizations.

☐ Attend community meetings.

Sharing Your Experience:

☐ Leave a review for your agent.

◻ Offer guidance or advice to others beginning their home buying journey.

Resources and References for Further Reading

Here are some resources and references for further reading on home buying and ownership:

Books:

"*Nolo's Essential Guide to Buying Your First Home*" by Ilona Bray J.D., Alayna Schroeder J.D., and Marcia Stewart: A *beginner's guide to the home buying process.*

"*The Book on Negotiating Real Estate*" by J Scott, Mark Ferguson, and Carol Scott: Expert strategies for getting the best deals when buying & selling investment properties.

"*Real Estate Investing For Dummies*" by Eric Tyson and Robert S. Griswold: A broad overview of real estate investment strategies.

Websites:

Realtor.com – Contains listings and advice on buying homes. It's backed by the National Association of Realtors.

Zillow.com – Besides property listings, Zillow offers

a range of resources including a blog with real estate advice and market trend data.

BiggerPockets.com – A comprehensive resource for real estate investors with forums, blogs, podcasts, and guides.

HUD.gov – The U.S. Department of Housing and Urban Development website has resources for homebuyers, including advice on financing and homeownership programs.

Organizations:

National Association of Realtors (NAR) – Offers a range of resources for homebuyers and information on the real estate industry.

National Association of Home Builders (NAHB) – Provides consumer information on home buying, construction, and renovation.

Real Estate Buyer's Agent Council (REBAC) – Offers resources on buyer representation and home buying strategies.

Online Courses and Webinars:

"The Homebuyer's Toolkit" on Udemy – This course covers the basics of buying a home from start to finish.

"Real Estate Basics" on Coursera – A course that delves into real estate concepts and provides foundational knowledge.

BiggerPockets Webinars – They frequently host webinars on a range of topics related to real estate investment.

Journals and Magazines:

"RealtyTrac" – Provides detailed listings, foreclosure data, and real estate trends.

"Real Estate Forum" – Covers industry news, trends, and best practices.

"HouseLogic" – Created by the National Association of Realtors, this site offers advice on home improvement, maintenance, taxes, finance, and insurance.

Glossary of Real Estate Terms

The world of real estate comes with its own language. To help you navigate this, here's a brief glossary of some commonly used terms:

Amortization: The process of spreading out a loan into a series of fixed payments. The loan is fully paid off at the end of this term.

Appraisal: An estimation of a home's market value by a licensed appraiser based on comparable recent sales of homes in the area.

Closing: The final step in the home buying process, where the property's title is transferred from the seller to the buyer.

Closing Costs: Expenses over and above the property price incurred by buyers and sellers when transferring property ownership.

Contingency: A clause in the contract that specifies conditions that must be met for the contract to be binding.

Down Payment: An upfront payment made by a buyer to secure the purchase of a property, typically ranging from 3-20% of the property's price.

Earnest Money: A deposit made by a buyer to a seller, representing a good-faith commitment to the property purchase.

Equity: The difference between the home's market value and the unpaid balance of the mortgage. It represents the owner's stake in the property.

Escrow: A neutral third party or account that holds funds for disbursal once conditions of a contract are met.

Fixed-Rate Mortgage: A mortgage with an interest rate that remains constant for the term of the loan.

Home Inspection: A comprehensive review of the property to check for defects or issues, often a contingency in the purchase agreement.

Listing: A written contract between an owner and a real estate agent, authorizing the agent to represent the seller and the property.

Mortgage: A loan taken out to buy property or land. The borrower agrees to repay the loan, plus interest, over a set term.

Pre-Approval: A lender's formal guarantee to grant a mortgage up to a specified amount.

Principal: The base amount of a loan, not including interest or additional fees.

Realtor: A real estate professional who is a member of the National Association of Realtors.

Refinancing: The process of getting a new mortgage, usually with a lower interest rate or to access equity, to replace the original loan.

Title: A legal document that proves ownership of a property.

Title Insurance: An insurance policy that protects against loss due to title defects or disputes.

Underwriting: The process by which a lender evaluates the risk of offering a mortgage to a homebuyer.

Zoning: Municipal or local government laws that dictate how certain geographic areas can be used.

This glossary provides definitions for some of the most common terms encountered during the home-buying process. However, the world of real estate is vast, and there are many more terms and nuances out there. It's always a good idea for readers to consult with professionals for any terms or concepts they're uncertain about.

.